poems

Sasenarine Persaud

We acknowledge the support of the Canada Council for the Arts for our publishing program. We also acknowledge support from the Government of Ontario through the Ontario Arts Council.

We acknowledge the financial support of the Government of Canada through the Canada Book Fund for our publishing activities.

Canadä

Cover design by Jaaron Collins
Author photograph by Denise Noone: Empire Cafe, Glasgow

Library and Archives Canada Cataloguing in Publication

Persaud, Sasenarine, 1958-, author
Love in a time of technology / Sasenarine Persaud.

Poems.
ISBN 978-1-927494-43-1 (pbk.)

I. Title.

PS8581.E7495L69 2014 C811'.54 C2014-902555-6

Printed and bound in Canada by Coach House Printing

TSAR Publications
P. O. Box 6996, Station A
Toronto, Ontario M5W 1X7
Canada

www.tsarbooks.com

Contents

Love in a Time of Technology

Elsewhere

Storm

Love in a Time of Technology

Love in a Time of Technology

And you will forget
how foxes yelped at night
near the Morningside Park
how mongrels roamed in packs
howling and barking
in a rage at spirits of the dark
fowl-cocks chain crowing
lighting up a foreday morning.
You are immersed in the Internet.
You have forgotten
how to speak, to say, "I'm sorry."
And you will part as you have met
through the portals of the Internet.

Love Within Love: Brookline Booksmith

Searching in the basement for a Palace
of the Peacock you find instead
a lookout on a hill overlooking
the Ottawa Valley, grass shimmering
like pages in your hand. Whose fingers
flipped these covers before revealing
the winter limbs of a writer's soul
full as pomegranate nipples tonight
can wait—upstairs a book sale;
we brush coats still damp
from the flurries outside and we are hungry
hungry hungry negotiating the book-bins.

Love Afterwards

Shaking with the tremors
of a distant plate shift
you will recall that library
touch of wrists erupting
from the space between our feet.
You will learn
earthquakes re-occur
anytime along the same fault
lines. And you can pace
in the same reading room
in a dozen different cities
in a thousand different ways
waiting for the same aftershocks:
the building has crumpled
the cars scream uncontrollably
dust rises from the rose garden
the iron chair is twisted
and you will ask
of every stranger you meet
among the broken concrete
how could this happen
how could this be.

Plane Tree

Pale limbs lifted
in a Florida room
of a summer evening
when fan blades whirl.

Pale arms aloft
offering nipples
swinging in the dusk
zebus going home
on a riverbank trail
for milking.

Orchids

Winter foliage burnt by frost
crackling and laughing
like a tropical bonfire
your leaves are browned hearts
your hearts are browned leaves
on the Indian orchid trees
transplanted from Asia.

You are looking
to Scotland or beyond China
to an American or Canadian
heartland for paper birch
while here in your own yard
the shrubs you both planted
dry before your eyes and still
make music waving limbs
as smooth as a zebu's
grazing in your South American
childhood. Look in your own pasture
look in your own yard
in your own house
on your own bed.

Hickson Park: Tampa on the River

I want to take you
where white lights
glow on deleafed winter
oaks like icicles,
where the dark river
floats a rubber slipper
inland—away from the bay
invading our souls,
where water erupts
under spotlights
like our love once
I want to take you
where laughter fills the night.

Take Back

Do not let April come
too quickly, or May—
take back your warmth
take back your buds
along the riverbanks
overlooking rapids cascading
milk on thighs—when
we closed our books, yet,
refusing to say goodbye.

The Tenth Love

Through floor-to-ceiling glass,
swaying oaks and nodding
elms give the lie to wall.
Beyond, the construction crane
is as still as a murti in the dusk.
Delivering so softly
even the microphone stretches
for amplification of souls on tongues—
a statistic once heard.
The average human falls in love
seven times during a lifetime.*
Only we are not average
you and I. We love once,
the same—not exactly—
multiple times, Meenawattie said,
deeper deeper deeper each time.

* With thanks to Katie Ford and her poem, "Koi."

Lighting the Dawn

In this silent morning
that your words unquiet
with Dante or Rome,
in the fruited morning,
when you rekindle
the eyes of Tess, her hand
orchestrating the air
and the landlord's daughter's tresses
and you must connect
the only way you can
across such spaces,
when thrush and mockingbird sleep
and you are sending a song
through this void of cyber spaces
a ping ignites our inboxes.

Gul-Gula*

Rolling down the Great Plain
in the Ganga delta,
an ancestor boarded in Kolkata.
The newly arrived from Chennai
marvelling at your kachourie:
Peppered dal encasing sliced cabbage
fried in Iowa corn oil. You left
the best for last. Double rose
balls flavoured with banana
blooming in your cheeks.

* An Indian sweetmeat

Vacations

Roosters announcing dawn
on the grass above the beach
from an island in paradise
you said. But who slept
at your side?
This couch is an Atlantic island
under fire, Sumter reduced to rubble:
the longest siege in modern warfare.

In park-ranger green and olive grey,
you perched on a stool near a cannon
above tourist heads, the south rising
from freckled neck to the wounded
silence of eyes a lemongrass flavour
in the Thai restaurant and rain outside
drowning out the distance, the years.

Hold My Hand

You will open your mouths
and these worlds will jump out;
hold my hand, hold my heart.
You will open mouths
and these histories will fly out
and around our throats
the air between our eyes
shimmering in a mirage
where the years evaporate
and the loves we touched
once, you will open your eyes
you will flip yellowing pages
and these worlds will jump out
I am here, I am now
hold my hand, hold my heart.

The Promise

The falling coin striking tiles
rolls into a corner
you have ceased looking at.
Where is the girl who gave
unreservedly, whose eyes held
promises you could not keep;
where is she whose silence
freed and trapped you
in a sub-tropical garden?
The fallen disc rests on cold ceramic—
your pocket is laden with plastic
that slide in and out of readers
accepting your promise to pay tomorrow—
is today a circle cartwheeling out of reach,
the apology wounding as much as it heals.

The Gathering

Throw your fingers in the air
and let them speak—
I would place vanilla on lips
toss your hair about
our eyes locking around talks
we will not have your calves
upon a sofa—there is no hair—
throw your fingers in the air
and let them speak our unspoken.

In Storage

Yellowing in albums
in cardboard boxes tucked
in a corner of Paradise a foot lifted
in motion a smile fading
in time silverfish—not those fish
in "forty-feet"—finding
more use for love's relics.

We send no letters.
An envelope is an antique.
In the digital world, we can almost
smell mangoes in Bourda Market
or hear parrots chattering
on the southern tip of a peninsula
but how does your hand
these days
shape a word or phrase
or embellish the flourish of a heart
at letter's end or an afterthought: PS

Here the personalities of pens
are imprisoned in sealed missives
in boxes
in images retreating along stuck edges
of soon-to-be consumed Kodak paper.

Fall Torrent

Turning away to raining words
fitting a year into an hour, monologues
on youth, again, laughing in the dark
at the fumbling with apparel
the fumbling with upside-down flesh.

When you want the quiet
of a hotel suite and I not
wanting to miss a second
of this look—twinkling eyes—
I need a little space, you say, please.

Walking up an autumn hill
in a refreshing chill, leaves falling
and calling come back come back
for dinner in an Indian restaurant
curry and dahi and rice, oil spills
on the tablecloth—crossing your legs
on a sofa and shaking a foot
like your father sated with Demerara spirits.

When you say, you are too narrow.
A gay is a human, too—or rather a mood
a state-of-childhood mind and there are stars
everywhere a gulf wind whisking away puffs
in a clear sky you want to dance
in a night-rain naked as clouds.

When you say it is not enough.
I want more than ephemera

more than you can give, quiet
in the morning's noanswernoresponse
and you are a parrot because there is
love and yet nolove across the distance
and the ponds of silence at departure.

Listening to Lata

Picking our way between
tall bamboos in a morning
ringed by New England hills
after another year elapsed
on a wick burning a decade
since that night your eyes igniting
a South American spark
plucked on sitar strings
Saraswattie's instrument wounding
the silence of all others
we loved and all who loved us.

Fifty and 50

All the things you said of fifty
at twenty were lies fed by fashion
and Holly-Bolly-wood.
Muscles are stronger
you know how to hear-not-hear
to let trifles go to trifle-land.

All the things you said of fifty
at thirty are phrases
you can't remember. At forty
you were busy looking for signs
of midlife crises that materialized
only in the books you didn't write.

At fifty you aren't thinking
of fifty; you are thinking
we will not write sonnets—
artificial forms on love; to be sure

Shakespeare was a hack
an Elizabethan Bollywood scriptwriter
who could teach you nothing
of an age he never attained: not Lear's
not Caesar's. Run a mile or two
at fifty, cycle twelve, kayak
on the Hillsborough River, cut the lawn
when it is over 100 degrees F outside
rekindle romances imagined at fifteen…

There are those who say come, come
act your age—who says, live your age?

Elsewhere

Elsewhere

The neighbourhood still sleeps
of a Sunday. The new AC unit
next door hums a morning raga.
Carolina wrens flute alongside
the insistent blue jays' questions:
why are you not in Toronto
or in Georgetown with no cares
except wanting to be elsewhere—
wanting to be in such a place
as you are right now, in Florida,
away and outside yourself.

One

One says one
is the fluttering of stars
at night in a dissolution
at morning; a wick turned down
until lit by dusk. One says
one is the yolking of lingum
and yoni—Shiva's flaming
in a fireside; but One says one
is not the same as one.

From Mouth to Ear

for Robert Pinsky

While the hall filled
To hear you speak
Of the word's magic
Moving from here to here
i.e. From mouth to ear—

I could have been a great musician,
(A sitarist—daddy played mandolin ragas)
But did not have the talent
So I decided to be a great poet—
We learned all there was to a question.
How do investors hedge bets
And precipitate a Great Recession?
Mutual funds, hedge funds and
Mortgage-backed securities are words.

What, then, is more important?
Substance or style, sound of words
Or sight? Both in equal measure.
Not putting down hip-hop,
Is there anything like jazz?

Anything at all in the world
Of punctured silence like the raag?
Some saying raga—
The prerogative of an American education.

A black cat stalking the dusk
And the concrete strip behind the podium
Does not seek admittance.

His primary concern's dinner—
Jesus of Nazareth had the luxury of supper.
In retrospect, they weren't seeing

How you make history. If only conquerors
Make history, poets are the greatest historians
Or the greatest conquerors. We settle
For both. Mesmerized in the moment,
In primordial sound—some call
AUM, or with the benefit of Englishes,
OM—we are applauding. The man
With the pencil moustache has a point—two.

Who hears anything after death?
I would rather hear it now: a poem request.
And yet we always hear. We always die
And always live. This, too, a lie.
At the congressional hearing,
Goldman Sachs is in the hot seat.
They hedged. They bet against themselves
And their clients. They caused the Great Recession.

You are listening to the Nazis.
The Swastika is an ancient Hindu thing
Of good fortune, which we cannot wear
In public. I cannot invite you to our puja
Where we outline this symbol on our altar
Bede. And, yet, here we are
Applauding fiercely—did you start with Namaste—
As you close your book.

You thank god all humans are not hedge fund
Managers. And you thank the poet for god:
In the beginning there was sound.
Some call that AUM and some OM.

Fireflies Caught in Molasses . . .

Derek Walcott

Where you found the goldsmith from Benares,
I heard a Pandit from Varanasi
a conch calling divine manifestations
to a South American puja
under a bael—goldenapple—tree

I must still translate for you,
for me, digital sadhus smeared
in a grey powder remaindered
from shells of exiled consciousness.

It is not fashionably correct to say, *I have*
little interest in Benin. The "I Man"
who immersed himself in Africa
did not need to provide explanations
for ancestral obsessions, and offered none.

Could you criticize a Kenyan or Ghanaian
search for roots? Yet "pseudo sadhus"
from Couva were fine according to a bronzesmith's
craft, or s/he who went to, or came from Oxford.
But the molasses created from that Indian cultivar
of grass—sugar-cane—trapping ants
and marabuntas and common houseflies

For us are tigers' eyes glowing in the night.

The Master's Hands Shake at a Reading

for Derek Walcott

Pages quiver like apple blossoms
in spring rain gathering the grass
to earth—lie down lie down,
place a glass laptop table before
my chair to steady fingers.

No warrior should come to this.
No Philoctetes scratching gangrenous leg,
no proud Achilles in a torn singlet
astride a little boat's bow
like Papa near Cuban inlets
celebrating in elegy these islands
in the stream, proud mountaintops,
will last forever and yet
the moon falls down into the sea
much like the sun in the dust
at dusk giving way to a teeth of stars.

In Our Heads

Fireflies light our heads
in an afternoon
when there are none
must be pre-festival fireworks
or the stars that light
journeys to other worlds.

A Taj Tale

She bore him fourteen children
in nineteen years. The favourite wife
of the harem, according to historians
of the victors, recorded long after.
She died in childbirth. They hid how

For one year the body languished
in a provincial grave
while the emperor appropriated
The Marble Wonder: Raja Jaisingh's
temple palace. It took twenty-two years

To build, Tavernier, the French jeweller
said, initiating another tale. He made four
trips to India. He was nowhere near Agra
in 1632, when he said he was
at the apparent start of construction.

How many diamonds did the mogul emperors
allow him to cart out of India? The emperors'
chroniclers do not say. The British Raj covered
his back. Even now, Cameron, a British PM
says: *We will not return the Kohinoor*

Diamond to India. They let him visit
New Delhi all the same. Twenty-two years
to convert a Shiva temple palace
to inscribe verses from an Arabic book
to overwrite and overlay native decorations.

You cannot take pictures of anything
inside, the Moslem guides say.

The emperor's son overthrew him.
From his prison cell,
the deposed mogul would only look
backward in a mirror at the Tejo-Mahalya.
It anguished his heart, the chroniclers say,
to look directly

At his theft from Mother India.

Storm

Storm

You brought me back
to Napoleon retreating
in snow falling
from Tolstoy's hand
liquor at Russian lips.

You brought me back
to crows circling
winter stormed Toronto
woods accepting a body's fall
and the poison at my mother's mouth.

Snow Kiss

For how you covered cracks
in sidewalks and puddled pavements
in summer minds—snowy ash
waving in a wind preceding hail
stinging rooftops and windscreen
wipers careering wildly in our eyes
we shoved aside and building up
at the corners and everywhere
filling in hollows where our sacred dead
lay buried and skeletoned and borrowed mice
cease nibbling at a slice of our discontent.

Near Bloor & Yonge

Snow dusting pavement
in a feather touch
at the intersection,
you pause, eyes skywards.
Who is looking down
on textured legs
on seeker's lips moving
towards your own
and the faraway voice
on a speaker phone
you will always take
to other cities: you have
edited out your voice
you have left your passion
at this junction—Britnell's
bookstore, The Bay, Manulife
named after an ancient Indian
lawgiver, you think—obsessions coated
by flurries embracing tempered glass.
You will return.
You will strum love songs.

Magnolia Plantation, South Carolina

Breaking the silence of months
we are touring old plantations;
that thing which brought us
west and north and south
robbing us of an inheritance—
famine or conquerors' histories.

This planter came from Barbados
and further back a contemporary
Shakespeare relative. One ancestor
was there when the world was made.

In the thunderstorm, we listen
to your eyes. The first building
caught fire in a storm. The second
burned at the end of the Civil War.

How? There were, are, Yankees
in the South—tourist dollars—rebels.
There were—are—the Southern
Suttees, would immolate themselves
rather than give up to the enemy.

Sumter: In Black and White

It was there rising from the Lowlands
grass as we motored in—what do you drive,
Japanese or Korean, everyone asked
on that other alluvial plain below sea level,
the Dutch West India Company
revelling in the fertile flatlands, mosquitoes
no strangers to Raleigh-seekers in the bush.

And it is here, too, as we cross the river
and the mudflats searching
for the tea plantation, the GPS changing
colours and adding a vowel "u"
is suicide in American letters—how
did Washington spell, using this language
from across the Atlantic—roads crumbling
in the Southern summer heat, rain pouring
during a stop at a lookout, where naval
vessels plied cannons flaying the fort.

It was here as we paused in the air
conditioned room, two men dressed
like dandies poised atop the rubble
and you have to look closely
at the photographs to ascertain their colour.

Kew Gardens, New York

Despite the buzz from the highway
and the earthquake cracks in the sidewalk,
horse chestnut, oak and maple roots
puncturing the pavement; despite the bearded
Middle-eastern-looking, phlegm-spitting
taxi driver stopping on this sleepy side
road to urine on the vined fence—I don't
disrespect your dead, or your great city,
I had to go—you come for your repeat
morning stroll. The German Shepherd barks,
in the lot behind the cemetery, after the departing
cab. And the cardinal still sings and spreads
his red robe across old tombs and oaks,
elms, dogwoods and maples—tree-hopping.

Cancer Patient Losing Voice

Waking in an overcast to an unmusical
ringtone, you are breathing like a bull
Krishna may have herded in Mathura

A voice from a Queens Borough
cold in January, calendars marking
another year's beginning and a prognosis

The eighty-year relative who dances
in summer dusks and plays cards
with nephews and drinks aged El Dorado

Rum in the humid New York nights
firing limbs until the doctor
postulates: it could be six months

Or sixteen. You hear too many voices
and none. You have too many tongues
and none. To celebrate the breath

Of he who blows into the ancient bansuri*
from California by the sea through
another relative singing: I was born

In the same year as D A Walcock.
True, I ain't win no Nobel Prize, but
I ain't dead yet. I still drinking rum
eating garlic-pork and playing Twenty-one.**

* An Indian bamboo flute
** Also another name for the card game, blackjack

Florida in March of the Great Recession

Mockingbirds are late
in coming. Jays and cardinals
stay away. Only wrens
and vultures remain
among burnt palms
and shrivelled hibiscus.

In a slash pine copse
there is frost
on the gables
frost on the grass
frost on house hips
mirroring the sky

A Great Recession
Sprinkling, like salt
on seared lawns,
"HOUSE FOR SALE" signs swaying
everywhere like July 4th decorations;
stars and tiger stripes littering the sky.

Gulfmusic

When stars joyed
in an inability to sleep—
before dark gold rushing
from the exploded Deepwater
Horizon lived up to its moniker;
before crude made landfall,
in a night when stars cavorted
and flesh lapped flesh on sand
and we did not have to think
about tar-balls, or rigs in the sea.

The Gazebo

The card reads: steel and aluminum
coated metal. Years of backyard
leisure. Rust gathers quickly
in creases where water clings
to grooves. The coated metal puffs
and flakes like the scales of a beached fish
falling off on Honeymoon Island.
Only the aluminum rivets are untouched
by decay, the discarded card reading:
Guaranteed to last. Made in China.

A Summer Frock

And you, lady, swirling
a peacock summer frock
over a peacock's strut,
where are we now,
lady, lipping first afternoons
kissing first autumn nights
brown black eyes shooting
spears across the river
spreading palms cannot hide
your tiny breasts' hunger
for Hollywood, lady,
love does not dissipate
when we learn of politics
or partners lady
love does not dissolve under
a swirling peacock frock of niceties.

A Leaf of Neem*

Like a catbird calls
of an evening
you want to hear your soul
or a thrush this morning
gurgling dreams
when you want to sleep later
what phrase was it we uttered
what poem spun off
the beak of rhetoric
drew tears from your heart
and lips clamped tight
on the years as if on a leaf of neem.

* The leaves of the neem tree, used in Ayurvedic medicine and as a natural insecticide, are bitter.

Wildflowers

Wilting in the Florida sun
white wildflowers were shapes
we'd never seen—starbursts
in the spring grass waving
goodbye hello no ants on shirt
no snake in the pond no turtle
surfacing for air no woodpecker
tap-dancing on a bark musicing our ears.

Daffodils

These daffodils that were not
Naipaul's or Walcott's, once foreign,
still smarting cane-stalk bruises
and lashes and histories we cannot see
hearts breathing on thin stalks—
these daffodils that are yours
uncorrupted by second guesses
or second lives are also mine today.

Tulips

And if in spring
I sing praises to tulips
instead of marigolds
daffodils instead of oleanders
or at my desk bite
an apple instead of a turmeric
mango—not concealed pleasure
on the side—it is because
I have no country
but the country of Gandhi's *Gita*[*]

[*] The Bhagavad Gita

Prelude to Bed: The Avocado

Avocadoes are not pears,
you said
with the authority of a PhD
from an American university,
Bartletts are
the shape of teardrops
defining that last parting—
do you still sleep naked
in the Florida dark?—
the Oxford English Dictionary
will not do as arbiter, invoking
the Internet and settling for Wikipedia;
the avocado is, after all, still a pear.

Morning at the Office

One walks a question
barefoot to your desk
an offering to eyes Snow White
hides from the sun. One walks
high on heels; good morning
says your name on a plastic
label on the wall. A greeting
is both professional and personal—
take it how you wish. One walks
eyes across partitions that are almost
non-existent. O really! I didn't
notice! And quickly sunlight stalks
across oaks outside your glass
walls and computers hum
a thousand songs unsung.

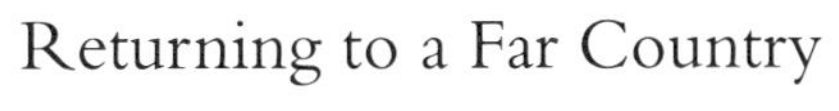

Returning to a Far Country

Returning to a Far Country

1.
Old fears reappearing
as you clear Customs
the mini-van-taxi drivers soliciting
beyond the fluorescent glare
armed soldiers mounted on a jeep
waiting for rebels
who vowed to disrupt your visit.

This is no movie from a couch.

Stars decorate the black beyond
the canefields and the checkpoint
with tyre-piercing barriers
alternating on the highway—
one car at a time let through
darkness to the city's edge.

A heavy-lidded sentry's
questions answered
lifts the hotel's barrier gate.
Light overwhelms the drop-off
through automatic glass doors
and the plantation still cultivated
here in your childhood.

2.
You have slept for two decades.

Dew lines the balcony rail
beyond which a draycart passes a cyclist.

Harness and hooves are a raga's alaap
carrying westward to the riverbank
where your grandfather hoisted you
on his lap singing chowpais
from Tulsidas' *Ramcharitmanas*—the Hindi
Ramayana—the longest poem
by a single poet! And you think
"The Homer of the Caribbean" greater!

That sound is no rooster's crowing
but a fowl-cock extending wings
to conceal spurs before mounting
A Rhode Island or Providence hen.
Marigolds cup the dawngold sunshine
and your driver announces his arrival,
on time, like a Prussian military officer.

3.
You are a tourist to the chauffeur,
a senior at the university: that
is the La Penitence Market—the French
designing much of the city; that
the Stabroek Tower where the Dutch
established a European outpost; that
Parliament Buildings, completed
by the British; here is the Campbellville
Car park—and you finally utter—
where my first love and I
waited in the rain for a taxi
before shedding our virginity—
and there was no greater rain
and there was no greater city
in no greater country
in no greater time
than this time of our love.

Dennis Street: Daddy

When you had a drink,
or two, or more you cursed
the tyrant President-for-life
in the foulest words. We revelled
in this new language
Mommy would have disapproved.

But you sang the sweetest filmi hits
of Mukesh on love and heartbreak
of that time in the fifties you married
and your mandolin plucked
the hearts of strangers and neighbours.
And you cried in the molasses dusk
falling silent, then staggering
to bed, "Lock up boys."

We knew her, then,
understood what she must have felt
putting up with you all those years
as we emptied the Goodyear tyre
ashtray, wiped the ice-bowl rings,
crated the coke empties, capped
the half-filled rum bottles
and switched off all lights
to conserve electricity.

Dennis Street: Carol

You are singing
all kinds of everything...
while the warm shower
water cascaded over limbs.
Red heels we saw
milked calves we saw
of a sandaled evening
under the mango tree
leaning over the trench
and a caiman lurking
beneath your white concrete bridge
leading to the only white
concrete house in the city.

We could revel in a tropic
about to be engorged
in a postcolonial ruler's appetite;
his envy giving way to grudges nursed
from a plantation childhood; beatings
giving way to murders and assassinations
we could not imagine from Bond
or mercenary movies set in Africa
playing at the Strand or Astor or Globe.
Or even in books, or ancestral genes.

All kinds of everything
you are still singing in the spring
showers, *summer time winter time*
spring and autumn too-oo . . .
We all fled, prowling the streets

of Manhattan under gingkoes
and Japanese cherries blooming
after the long chill, marvelling
at mannequins—as you have, too—
frozen in storefront windows
faceless and, almost, raceless.

Dennis Street: The Guru

Rain falling and divesting
the gravel street of dust.
The sarod* master, picking
a way around puddles no different
from his monsooned city
to fulfill a contract for three years
teaching how to pluck sitar strings
in an outpost of Indian civilization
in South America, turning up at our door.
Forgetting ancient relationships guru-ji,
I could not wash your feet, or invite you in,
place you on a cherished seat.
I could not offer you tea—we had
none. The dictator banning that, too.

* An Indian stringed instrument

Dennis Street: The Fright

There was that lemon fridge
which represented the fifties
daddy would not throw away—
it worked with kerosene
before being outmoded
by electricity—until, as niche
for hide and seek, it locked
with you inside screaming
until white, until a neighbour
broke the latch just in time. The fifties
and the last remnant of mommy,
daddy must have thought,
were taken away the next day.

Mamoo

Turning, you shot the steel-tipped arrow
through the target, through the flattened
steel-drum-fence: "I expected more."
Brother of mother, friend of father
surrogate parent, porknocker come home
with a gifted set of the finest
Amerindian arms we'd ever seen,
held: long bow, short bow, metal tipped
and wood tipped arrows guided by eagle
feathers: the wood is for shooting fish,
the iconic image on a British Guiana
postage stamp sent the world over.

Behind your gift, the reason you always
returned to the interior was an Amerindian
girl—beautiful in my boy's mind that day
she came to the city knocking the steel gates.
Knocking and pausing, knocking and waiting.
"Leslie live here?" she asked. I nodded.
I let her in. I let her out. What transpired
between her and granny: *he's not home.*
I will not have a "buck" daughter-in-law.

She walked away in the dust haze
rising from Dennis Street, unpaved then.
I saw no water in her eyes, no tears. I've
always wondered what she saw in mine as
she nodded. They say she bore you a son.

You never married. There were other

women. We heard whispers, until
that Christmas Party, that taking off and
"living home" with another man's wife—
and Granny no daughter-in-law by you.

We no longer care for a wider world's fame
or gold and diamonds you garnered in the bush.
After all these years, when I return, you say:
"I expected more from you. I expected more
from you." Twice, as if I didn't hear the first.

I've never said, not once: Did you know, Mamoo,
an Amerindian girl came searching for you.

Old Colonial Bandstand, Georgetown

Curved and triangulated edges
the Raj might have borrowed
from the roofs of Rajput palace forts
or the roofs of Rajput palace temples—
as the Moguls did—romancing history
Victorian structures on South American
seashores, where of a Saturday evening
the regimental band offered classics.

We touched hands. We touched lips
in the salted air, the ocean spray
decorating spectacles: youth would last
forever and love and love's feet
floating on clean concrete
laid on a wall designed by the departed Dutch.

The view across the Atlantic
is obscured by billboards
and stars appearing in the dusk
with cinematic sex, paint peeling
from metal railings. The urine
stench mixed with feces
overpowering the cologne seaspray.

And the shirtless man fixing his bundle
on the Victorian pavilion is unnoticed
by the beachgoers. You avert your eyes.
You have not returned to find failings,
to look at sores, or unattended rag
bundles holding all of a life, and the shout
of waves: at the end you are alone—alone, alone.

Home

And you acquiesced
like broken Dasaratha
father, as she freighted us
with dreams in the bottomhouse:
Go out into the world
go over the vast oceans
cross strange rivers like Rama.

You didn't tells us about Ravana,
exile's ten-headed demon
seizing our other selves
and laughing at the gods in battle:
you will win back part of yourself
and yet lose all
when you return
it will not be the same

Home is everywhere and nowhere.

Georgetown

For evenings on the seawall
drinking soup thickened with coconut milk,
melting cassava, sweet potatoes and plantains;
for your smile in the mornings, a wave
from your platform as we pass, the trade wind
in our faces; for roasted peanuts jumping
out fingers unto sand and breakers exploding
on old brick groynes jutting into the Atlantic's
belly and tempering tides as stars flick on;
for conversations on galaxies, or monologues,
what if we are from beyond beyond,
aliens in this space and the ocean spray
sprinkling spectacles and moistening lips;
for a first kiss, or second riding around
the bandstand, the dance of street lights
in your eyes, I would return. I would dare all
gun-wielding bandits to walk, linked fingers
with your ghost on the sapodilla brown sand.

In Golden Years

And if such time should ever come
when body slows down
and limbs feel like lead,
let me not journey
like an investment banker
still travelling through a flush
of derivatives in a Great Recession;
let fingers somersault like orangutans
let words burnish stars on tongues
let adjectives flame on stone lingums.

Notes

Orchids: The Indian orchid tree, with its heart-shaped leaves, is sacred to many Indians for its association with Krishna. It grows to 50 feet and blooms in the winter. It has been planted in many parts of Florida.

Listening to Lata: Lata Mangeshkaris regarded as the greatest Indian play-back singer of all times. Saraswattie's Instrument—the Vina, which looks like a sitar, is perhaps the oldest known stringed instrument. Saraswattie is the Goddess of learning & knowledge.

One: Shiva as the Nataraja is shown dancing in a ring of fire, the eternal fire of dissolution and creation. In the Hindu trinity of Brahma, Vishnu and Mahesh, Shiva (Mahesh) is the God of Dissolution. The lingum is a symbol of Shiva in the form of the flame/fire of dissolution. Subsequent depictions added a yoni, or (oil) vessel in which the flame is centered, sustaining the flame. There are also interpretations and depictions of the Shiva lingum and yoni as the male organ resting on the female's.

Losing Your Voice: Krishna is considered an incarnation of Vishnu. Bansuri—a bamboo flute, the instrument of Krishna. DA Walcock—Derek Walcott has referred to VS Naipaul as VS Nightfall in one of his poems.

Home: Dasaratha in the *Ramayana* is the father of Rama, the hero of the *Ramayana,* who is regarded as an incarnation of Vishnu. Because of a promise given to Kaikeyi, Dasaratha had to send Rama into to exile for 14 years, just as he was about to make Rama crown-prince. Ravana is the villain in the *Ramayana* who abducts Sita, the wife of Rama.

Fireflies Caught in Molasses: Puja, a prayer ceremony, worship.

A Taj Tale: Some researchers in the last 50 years have shown that it is a myth (but still accepted as fact) that the Taj Mahal was constructed by Shah Jahan, a Mogul/Muslim ruler, as a love memorial to his favorite wife, who died giving birth to her 14th child (in 16 years). Even India's celebrated Nobel Laureate, Rabindranath Tagore, believed the lie of the history of the Taj. The official history of the Taj claims that construction of the Taj commenced in 1632 and took 22 years and involved 20,000 people. The first mention of these dates and figures is by the French jewel trader, J B Tavernier, in his book on his trips to India, which was published in 1675. Tavernier, who made 6 trips to India, claimed he was in Agra when construction was begun and completed. However, analyses of Tavernier's trips (detailed in Dr V S Godbole's book, *Taj Mahal: Simple Analysis of a Great Deception*) cross-referencing the dates Tavernier visited Indian cities show that this is a fabrication.

Mamoo: Mamoo—maternal uncle. A porknocker is a term used for a prospector for gold and diamonds in the Guyana bush. It is unclear exactly how the term porknocker came to be applied to the prospectors but there are two plausible explanations. One is that these prospectors had to take all their food, consisting of salted pork, into the bush with them. Another is that the prospectors were often so broke that when they arrived at the settlements and outposts, they would have to scrape, or knock, the bottoms of the empty wooden barrels for scraps. A porknocker of Indian ancestry was a rarity.

Acknowledgements

To *The Toronto Quarterly* in which "Near Bloor & Yonge" first appeared;

To *Wasafiri* (Issue No 73, Spring 2013) in which the following poems appeared: "Returning to a Far Country".

To *South Asian Ensemble* (Vols. 3 & 4, Winter 2012) in which "Orchids", "Home", "Hickson Park: Tampa on the River" and "The Tenth Love" were published

To *Muse India* (Issue 41, 2012, Hyderabad) in which the following appeared: "Love in a Time of Technology", "Love Afterwards", "Visiting the Taj" and "Fifty and 50".

Brookline Booksmith for selecting and publishing "Love within Love."

To Liza Greig and the BBC for publishing and broadcasting 'Georgetown' as part of the BBC's Poetry Postcard project celebrating the Commonwealth Games in Glasgow (summer 2014).

To Kavita Ramdya for the line "Love in a Time of Technology" from her review of *In a Boston Night*.

Denise Noon

Sasenarine Persaud is an essayist, novelist, short-story writer, and poet. He is the author of ten books: seven poetry collections, two novels, and a book of short stories. He was born in Guyana and has lived for several years in Canada. He has served as a vice-president and chair of the membership committee of the League of Canadian Poets, on the Board of Directors of the Scarborough Arts Council (Toronto), and on juries for the Toronto Arts Council and the Ontario Arts Council. He presently resides in Tampa, Florida.